D1367758

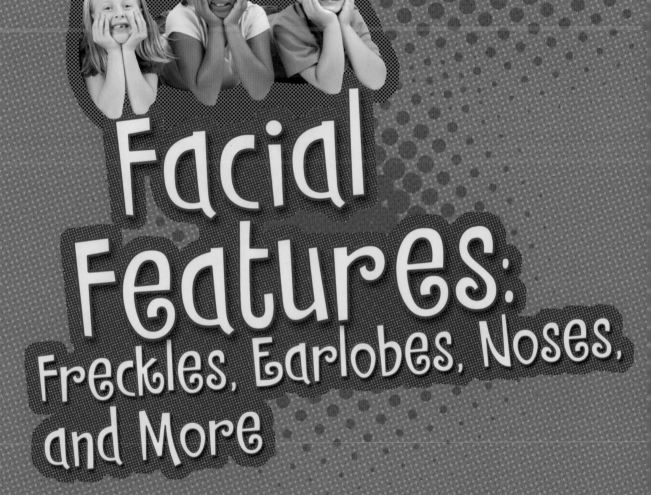

LIGHTNING BOLT BOOKS™

Facial Features:
Freckles, Earlobes, Noses, and More

Jennifer Boothroyd

Lerner Publications Company

For Essia and her
dazzling smile

—J.B.

Lerner Publications Company
A division of Lerner Publishing Group, Inc.
241 First Avenue North
Minneapolis, MN 55401 U.S.A.

Website address: www.lernerbooks.com

Library of Congress Cataloging-in-Publication Data

Boothroyd, Jennifer, 1972–
    Facial features : freckles, earlobes, noses, and more / by Jennifer Boothroyd.
        p.   cm. — (Lightning bolt books™—what traits are in your genes?)
    Includes index.
    ISBN 978–0–7613–8939–2 (lib. bdg : alk. paper)
    1. Face—Juvenile literature. I. Title.
    QM535.B66 2013
    611'.92—dc23   2011042018

Manufactured in the United States of America
1 — CG — 7/15/12

Table of Contents

Traits

Look at the people around you. They all have eyes, ears, and noses. People have a lot in common!

All people have the same basic parts.

But you can tell people apart.

It's easy to tell these best friends apart.

Traits help us tell people apart.
Traits are differences
between people.

Brown hair is a trait.
So are blue eyes.

Genes tell your body how to make different traits. Genes are like instructions for the body.

We all have different genes. But people have more genes in common with one another than they do with dogs or other animals.

Our birth parents gave us our genes.

Birth parents are related to their children. Adoptive parents take a child into their family and become his or her parents.

You have two copies of each of your genes. One copy came from each parent. The copies are called alleles. Sometimes you need two of the same allele to get a trait. Other times, you need just one allele.

You need two red-haired alleles to have red hair.

Freckles

Many traits are found on your face.

Look closely at your face. Its appearance comes from your genes.

Freckles are a trait. Freckles are spots on the skin.

Pigment makes freckles.
Pigment gives skin its color.
It's spread out in those without
freckles. It's clumped together in
those with freckles.

Do you have
freckles?

It takes just one freckle allele to give a person freckles.

This girl has a freckle allele.

Ear Traits

Look at the bottoms of these ears. Can you tell how they are different?

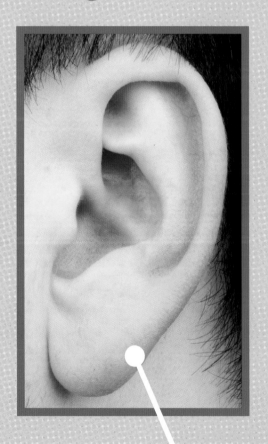 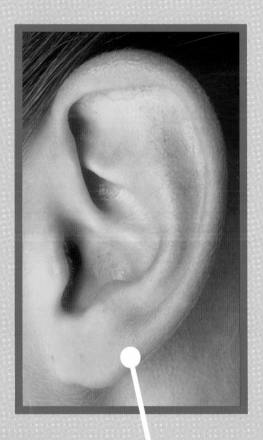

The bottom part of the ear is called the earlobe.

Some people have earlobes that hang away from their face.

Other people have earlobes
that are attached.

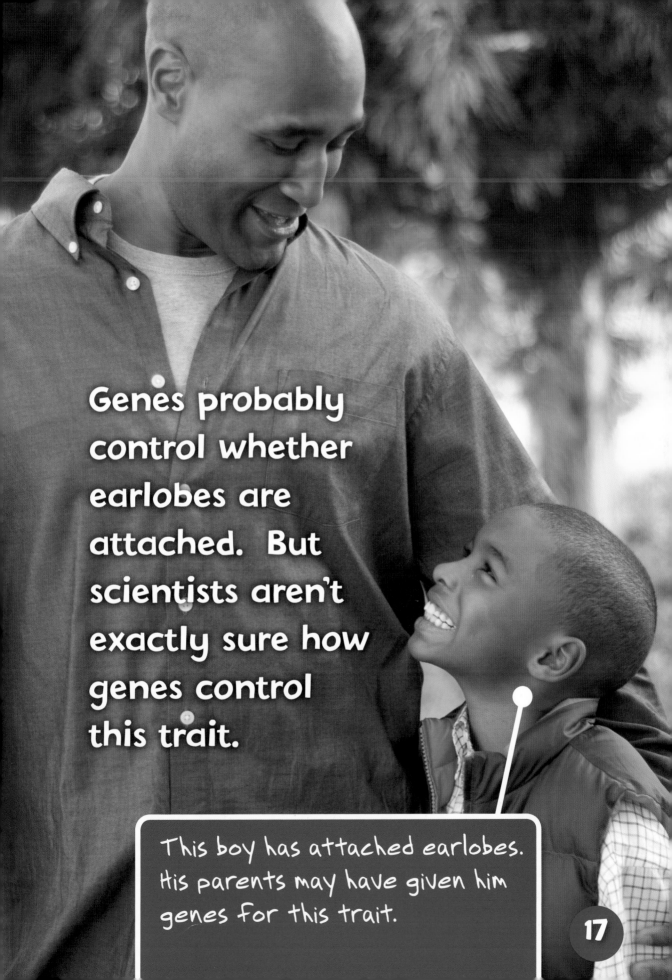

Genes probably control whether earlobes are attached. But scientists aren't exactly sure how genes control this trait.

This boy has attached earlobes. His parents may have given him genes for this trait.

Ears with a pointed tip are another ear trait. Genes might control this trait too. But again, scientists aren't sure how.

This ear's pointed tip is called Darwin's ear point.

Nose Traits

Noses come in many shapes. Genes help decide the shape of your nose.

This mother and daughter have similar noses.

Some noses are big.
Some are small.

These friends' noses aren't exactly the same.

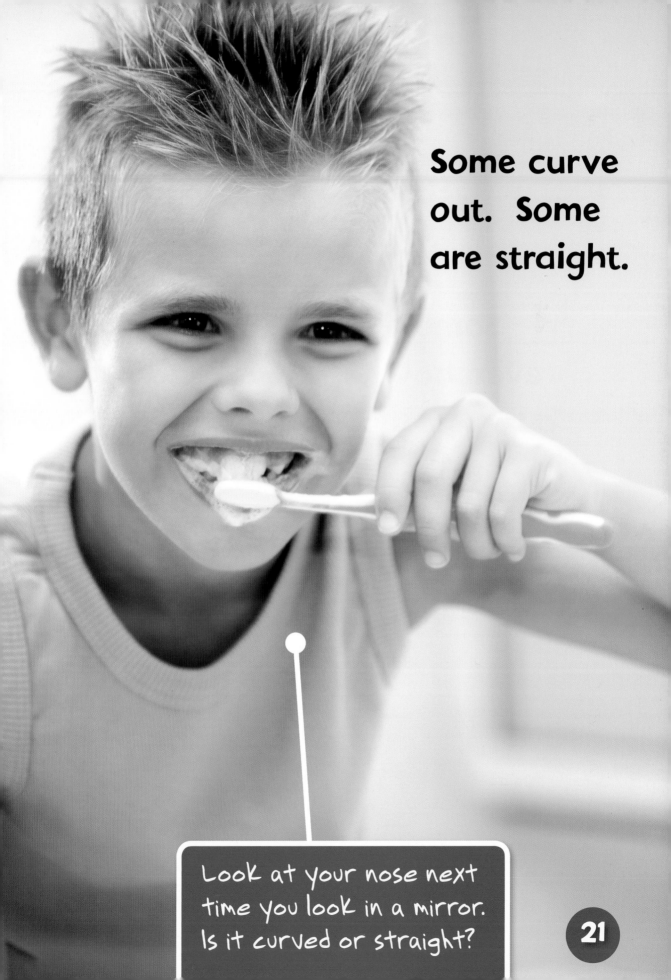

Some curve out. Some are straight.

Look at your nose next time you look in a mirror. Is it curved or straight?

Some
even have
a turned-up
end.

A turned-up nose is
sometimes called a
button nose.

Fantastic Faces

There are many more traits you can see on the face.

Dimples are one.

Dimples are small dents in a person's skin. This child has dimples on her cheeks.

Cleft chins are another.

A cleft chin has a crease down the middle.

Large front teeth are
a trait too.

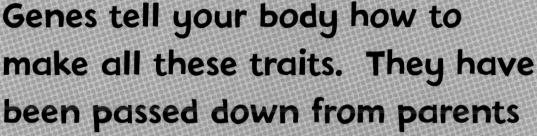

Genes tell your body how to make all these traits. They have been passed down from parents to children for generations.

What traits were passed down to you?

Activity
Track the Traits!

Track the facial features in your classroom. List these features on a sheet of lined paper:

cleft chin	hanging earlobes
no cleft chin	freckles
dimples	no freckles
no dimples	turned-up nose
attached earlobes	no turned-up nose

Then divide your paper into two columns. One column will be for the facial features. The other column will be for tally marks. (You'll find out what tally marks are and how to use them next.) Your paper should look like the sample sheet on page 29 when you're done.

Put a tally mark next to each facial feature that you have. A tally mark is a straight up-and-down line, like this:

|

Then ask your classmates about their features. Make a tally mark for each classmate next to his or her facial features. When you get to five, put a diagonal line through your tally marks, like this:

That's how you write the number five in tally marks. For the number six, make a new tally mark, like this:

When you're done tallying the facial features, count how many of you have each feature. Which features got the most tallies?

Sample Sheet:

Facial Features	Tally Marks
cleft chin	
no cleft chin	
dimples	
no dimples	
attached earlobes	
hanging earlobes	
freckles	
no freckles	
turned-up nose	
no turned-up nose	

Glossary

allele: one of two or more forms of a gene

birth parent: a parent who is genetically related to his or her child

cleft chin: a chin with a crease down the middle

dimple: a small dent in a person's skin

earlobe: the bottom part of the ear

freckle: a small, light brown spot on your skin

gene: one of the parts of the cells of all living things. Genes are passed from parents to children and determine how you look and the way you grow.

pigment: a substance that gives color to something

trait: a quality or characteristic that makes one person or thing different from another

Further Reading

American Museum of Natural History: The Gene Scene
http://www.amnh.org/ology/genetics#

The Geee! in Genome
http://nature.ca/genome/04/041/041_e.cfm

Harris, Trudy. *Tally Cat Keeps Track*. Minneapolis: Millbrook Press, 2011.

Klingel, Cynthia, and Robert B. Noyed. *Nose*. New York: Gareth Stevens, 2010.

Silverman, Buffy. *Body Parts: Double-Jointedness, Hitchhiker's Thumb, and More*. Minneapolis: Lerner Publications Company, 2013.

Tour of the Basics: What Is a Trait?
http://learn.genetics.utah.edu/content/begin/traits/tour_trait.html

Index

Photo Acknowledgments

The images in this book are used with the permission of: © iStockphoto.com/ Christopher Futcher, p. 1; © Blend Images/Ariel Skelley/the Agency Collection/Getty Images, p. 2; © Monkey Business Images/Dreamstime.com, pp. 4, 23; © Alija/the Agency Collection/Getty Images, p. 5; © Creasource/Canopy/CORBIS, p. 6; © LWA/ Photographer's Choice/Getty Images, p. 7; © iStockphoto.com/Ann Marie Kurtz, p. 8; © Jennifer Garske, p. 9; © iStockphoto.com/knape, p. 10; Leah Warkentin/Design Pics/ Newscom, p. 11; © Tomas Rodriguez/Ivy/CORBIS, p. 12; © Pam McLean/Brand X Pictures/ Getty Images, p. 13; © Zurijeta/Shutterstock.com, p. 14 (left); © Will & Deni McIntyre/ Photo Researchers/Getty Images, p. 14 (right); © Sabine Duerichen/LOOK/Getty Images, p. 15; © FB STUDIO/Alamy, p. 16; © Todd Wright/Blend Images/Getty Images, p. 17; © neal and molly jansen/Alamy, p. 18; © Edyta Pawlowska/Dreamstime.com, p. 19; © Terrie L. Zeller/Shutterstock.com, p. 20; © Cecile Lavabre/Photographer's Choice/ Getty Images, p. 21; © Sharon Dominick/Photodisc/Getty Images, p. 22; © Jason Weddington/Flickr/Getty Images, p. 24; © Leland Bobbe/Photodisc/Getty Images, p. 25; © PT Images/Shutterstock.com, p. 26; © iStockphoto.com/Mark Bowden, p. 27; © George Doyle/Stockbyte/Getty Images, p. 30; © Tatiana Grozetskaya/Dreamstime. com, p. 31.

Front cover: © joSon/Iconica/Getty Images.

Main body text set in Johann Light 30/36.